John Such

Cornwall

Landscapes

Bedruthan Steps.

John Such

Cornwall
Landscapes

DB PUBLISHING

Acknowledgements

I would like to thank the following people: Richard Elwell at Elburydesign.com for all my corporate design and art direction, but mostly for his valued friendship; DB Publishing for recognising my talent and signing me for this book and others in the future; Keith Appleby, my photography tutor over 25 years ago; and I would also like to thank Hel, Bex & Ems, the three ladies in my life! Finally, I want to thank all of my friends, family and clients who have supported me over the years.

John Such, 2010

An ancient tree at Trelissick gardens.

First published in Great Britain in 2010 by The Derby Books Publishing Company Limited, 3 The Parker Centre, Derby, DE21 4SZ.

© John Such, 2010.

A catalogue record for this book is available from the British Library.

ISBN 978-1-85983-801-3
Printed and bound by Progress Press, Malta.

Apple blossom.

An apple orchard near Truro.

The sun shines through the autumn leaves.

Introduction

Cornwall is a land of hidden beauty combined with the magic of Celtic myth. It has the longest coastline in the UK, featuring over 300 beaches. Glorious surfing beaches on the north coast contrast with sheltered beaches and delightful coves on the south coast.

Cornwall enjoys a pleasant climate all year round, allowing sub-tropical gardens to bask in long sunny days with waters warmed by the Gulf Stream. Great expanses of open moorland, hidden valleys and woodland, combined with dramatic skies and superb light, all make for great photographs.

For over 60 years film directors have used Cornwall as a backdrop for films, commercials and television programmes. Long-running series such as *Poldark* and, more recently, *Doc Martin* have all captured the hidden charm and beauty of this wonderful county.

Living and working in the South West helps you to appreciate the diversity it offers. Landscape photography requires patience, but when the light and subject matter work together there is no better feeling than capturing that moment. I like the thought process behind taking photographs, and the most important thing is that the shot has to be the best I can get from each situation. In this book I have selected a varied mix of images showing the beauty, lifestyle, history and quirks that make Cornwall the unique place that it is. I hope these images give you all as much pleasure as I have had in taking them.

An artist paints the coastline near Nare Head.

A bike for hire above the harbour in St Ives.

Camel bike trail near Padstow.

Whitewashed cottages in St Mawes.

Boats in Mylor
harbour at dusk.

Boats in Coverack.

Boats moored up in Newquay harbour.

Opposite: A river runs through a wooded valley near Cardinham, Bodmin.

The lookout tower at North Fistral.

A beautiful summers day at Gwithian.

Looking out across the sands to Nare Head.

Colourful flowers above the sea near Fistral, Newquay.

Cliff-top flowers at Tolcarne Beach, Newquay...

...and on Porth Island.

Seagull and family on the cliff edge near Port Isaac.

The clock tower at
Kingsand.

A view from the coastal path from Par to Polkerris.

The coastal path through the dunes at Holywell Bay.

The way to Nare Head.

The Redhill Down Walk
is a popular route on
Bodmin Moor.

A fishing boat moored up on the Camel Estuary near Padstow.

Colourful flowers in the dunes at Par.

Sailing boats on the Camel Estuary.

Polzeath beach on a summer evening.

Enjoying the view in St Mawes.

A secluded cove near Coverack.

An old stone wall on Bodmin Moor.

Rolling hills near Wadebridge.

A crisp winter morning at Pentewan, near St Austell.

Looking over to Ferryside, one of the homes where Daphne Du Maurier lived.

Cubert church.

The dawn sea at Marazion, near Penzance.

Colourful railings above Tolcarne beach in Newquay.

The Cornish flag flying in Mousehole.

Launceston Castle dominates its surroundings.

Early morning surf on Porthmeor Beach, St Ives.

Looking across the dunes at Par.

Dusk on Watergate Bay, near Newquay.

Enjoying the view at Harlyn Bay.

A summer evening on Perranporth beach.

Boats in the harbour at Coverack.

A Looe gardening club
display.

Pentire Head in Newquay.

A fishing boat heading in to Portloe.

Cruising up the river in Fowey.

Opposite: Fireworks over St
Austell Bay.

The footpath leading to
Gwithian beach, with
Godrevy Lighthouse in
the distance.

The sands of Watergate Bay.

Godrevy Lighthouse.

Gorse on Bodmin
Moor.

The summer sky.

Looking over to Newquay. .

Gull Rock at Whipsiderry.

Reeds growing on the lake in Par.

Left: A gold leaf perches at Golitha Falls.

Right: Golitha Falls.

Mexico Towans near Gwithian.

Hawkers Cove.

Pentire Headland.

A copse of trees covers the hill fort near Looe.

Looking out from Helman Tor.

A windswept tree at Helman Tor.

A rock formation on Helman Tor.

Sunset over Porth Island.

Sunset at Holywell Bay.

Fishing boats in Mevagissey harbour.

Holywell Bay.

Walking in Holywell Bay.

Sand dunes on Holywell Bay.

Watergate Bay.

The surging tide.

A surfer amid the breakers.

Above and left: A kitesurfer in full flow.

A lifeguard on the lookout.

A lonely tree on Bodmin Moor.

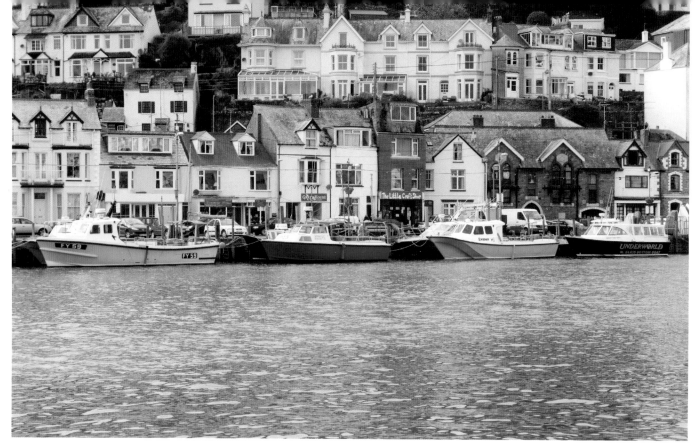

Moored up off West Looe.

The local fishmongers.

Looking up the north coast towards Tintagel.

49

Holiday chalets perch above the
sea at Freathy, Whitsand Bay.

The ancient site of Men an Tol.

A perfect summers day at Mexico Towans, Hayle.

On the creek in Gweek, Helston.

Boats moored in Padstow harbour.

Boats moored in Mousehole.

Offshore surf in Newquay Bay.

Looking out to Stepper Point.

The surf breaks against rocks at Porthcurno.

A summer bike ride on the north coast.

A Cornish stone wall near Porthtowan.

One of the best located B&Bs
in Cornwall!

Pampas grasses at
Pil Creek, Feock.

The dunes at Par.

Looking along the coast on a crisp winter morning in Pentewan.

Dune grass at Holywell Bay.

A dynamic advertisement for shark trips!

Rope by the harbour side.

Humourous advertising outside a boarded-up cafe in Newquay.

Big surf in Porthleven.

The Cribbar.

Opposite: The surf rolls in at Porthleven.

North Fistral.

An offshore breaker at North Fistral.

The cliff edge overlooking Newquay Headland.

Surf photographer Geoff Tydeman.

Opposite: European surf champion Ben Skinner surfing the Cribbar.

The popular surfing beach at Polzeath.

Opposite: The tiny bay of Polkerris.

Looking out from New Polzeath.

Pentire Point, New Polzeath.

Pentire Point in shadow.

Looking out from Porth Island.

The view from Porth Island to
Watergate Bay.

The busy Porthleven harbour.

Boats at Portscatho.

Looking out over Portreath.

The Red Arrows in perfect formation over Fowey.

The Red Arrows over Fowey.

Old petrol pumps in St Mawes.

Whitsand Bay with Rame Head in the distance.

The mystical Roche Rock.

Reflections in Mylor harbour.

Respryn Woods.

Another view of Bedruthan Steps.

The majestic
Bedruthan Steps.

Rolling hills near Pentewan.

Picturesque cottages in Kingsand.

Dappled sunlight in Bluebell
Woods, Ruthernbridge.

Sailing on the Camel Estuary.

Sand ripples.

Sea pinks.

A seagull in Fowey.

Seals being fed in Newquay harbour.

Holiday cottages in Charlestown.

A cove near Little Fistral.

The sun shines down on Prideaux House, Padstow.

Pencarrow House.

Looking out to sea at Pentewan.

A square-sailed ship moored off Charlestown.

St Austell Church.

St Michael's Mount rises out of the sea off Penzance.

Storm clouds approaching over Bodmin monument.

The china clay pyramid at Carclaze.

High tide in the village of Rock.

Moored up for lunch in Padstow.

Heading off for a summer surf session.

Surfing at Harlyn Bay.

Surfing at Great Western beach.

After another great day's surfing.

Surfers and their transport.

Sunset over Widemouth Bay, near Bude.

The sun setting on the
north coast.

Watergate Bay at sunset.

Sheep Dip Gully at Gwithian.

Waiting for sunset at New Polzeath.

Sunset over Porth Island.

Looking out over Padstow harbour.

Above and right: Thatched cottages in St Mawes.

A pretty window display in Port Isaac.

Teacups hanging in St Clement, Truro.

The famous Eden Project.

Truro Cathedral reaches skyward.

A view of Truro.

The Hurlers stone circle on Bodmin Moor.

The Hurlers stone circle on Bodmin Moor.

Derelict tin mines at Wheal Coates.

The Lookout at Kingsand.

Tolcarne beach in the summer.

A quirky sign at Daymer Bay.

Below and Opposite: Beach huts on Tolcarne beach.

HUT
HOLDERS
ONLY

Trees in a valley near Port Isaac.

Tropical seas in St Austell Bay.

Sunset over Gull Rocks.

Gull Rocks in Holywell Bay.

A Union Jack-painted pub in Saltash.

A pretty bus shelter in Cawsand.

An unusual sign on
Bodmin Moor.

Veryan Roundhouse.

A view of Padstow.

Portreath at high tide.

A view of Kingsand.

The Flat Rocks, Porth.

The romantic ruins
on Roche Rock.

Looking over to Rock.

Zacry's Island can be found between Whipsiderry and Watergate Bay.

The incoming tide.

The cruise ship *The World* moored in Fowey.

The Daymark at Gribbin head, Fowey.

A cruise liner waiting to berth in Fowey.

Paddling at Porth.

Dusk at Stem Point.

Looking over the
water's edge to
Whipsiderry.

The view out to Porth Island.

Offshore winds.

Opposite: Bodmin Moor.

Off for an autumn stroll.

A pretty window box in Kingsand.

Yachting off the north coast.

Hello campers!

Dusk on Charlestown beach.

A stack of lobster pots.

Sea urchins.

Pebbles on the beach at Charlestown.

Rape seed flourishing near Rialton.

The summer crop in Tregorrick.